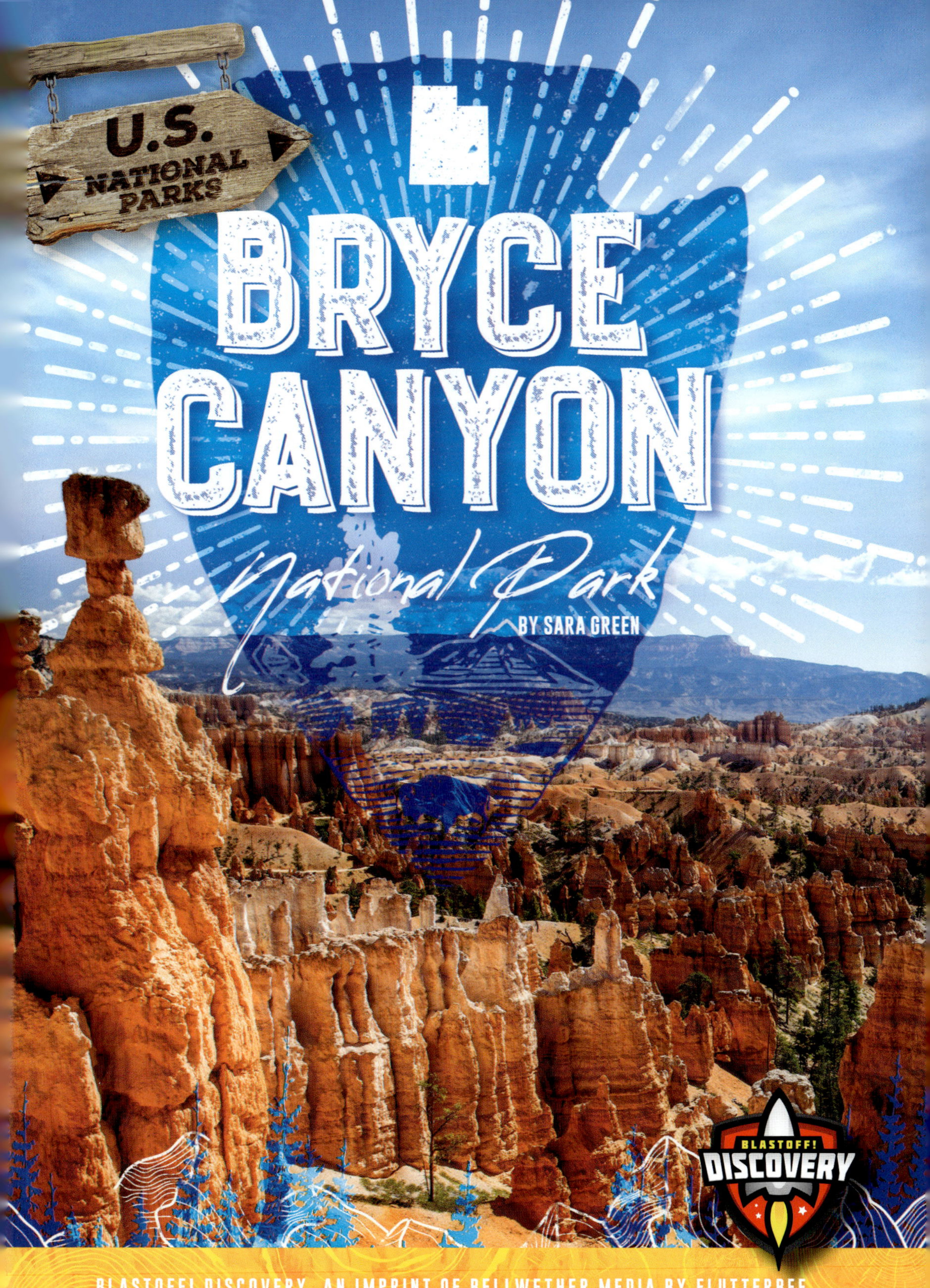

BLASTOFF! DISCOVERY, AN IMPRINT OF BELLWETHER MEDIA BY FLUTTERBEE

Blastoff! Discovery launches a new mission: reading to learn. Filled with facts and features, each book offers you an exciting new world to explore!

This edition first published in 2026 by Bellwether Media, Inc.

For information regarding permission, write to Bellwether Media, Inc., Attention: Permissions Department, 3500 American Blvd W, Suite 150, Bloomington, MN 55431.

Library of Congress Cataloging-in-Publication Data is available at www.loc.gov or upon request from the publisher.

ISBN: 9798893048469 (hardcover)
ISBN: 9798893049466 (ebook)

Editor: Elizabeth Neuenfeldt Designer: Laura Sowers

Printed in the United States of America, North Mankato, MN.

TABLE OF
CONTENTS

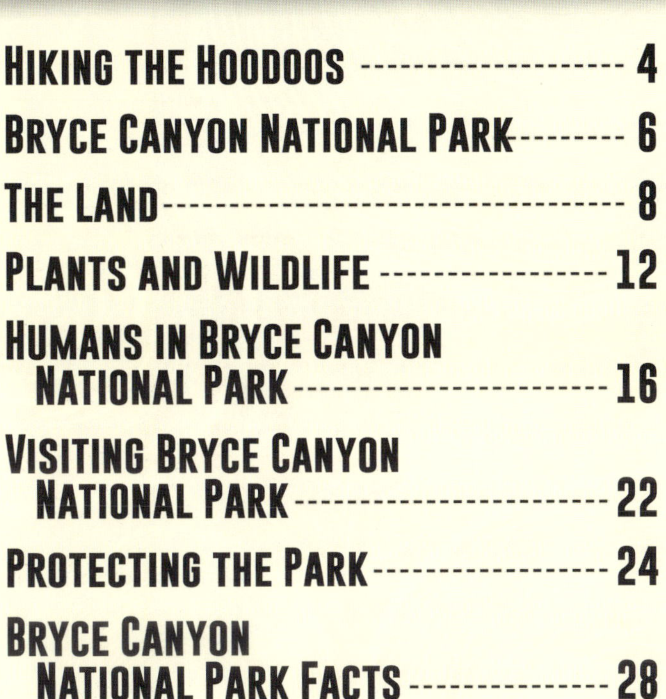

NATIONAL
PARK
SERVICE
BRYCE
CANYON
NATIONAL PARK
UNITED STATES
DEPARTMENT OF THE INTERIOR
NATIONAL PARK SERVICE

HIKING THE HOODOOS

A family arrives at Bryce **Canyon** National Park in Utah. They are excited to see rock formations called **hoodoos**! First, the family drives to a scenic overlook. It offers a sweeping view of the Bryce **Amphitheater**. Red and orange hoodoos spread across the landscape!

Next, the family hits the trail. The Navajo Loop trail leads them to Thor's Hammer, the park's most famous hoodoo. Back at the Visitor Center, the family reserves a spot for the night's **telescope** program. They will see countless stars in the sky!

BRYCE CANYON NATIONAL PARK

Bryce Canyon National Park has the most hoodoos in the world. The park is in southwestern Utah. It covers around 56 square miles (145 square kilometers), making it one of America's smallest national parks.

Bryce Canyon is not actually a canyon. It is a series of amphitheaters carved into a **plateau**. Park **elevations** range from 6,600 feet (2,012 meters) at its lowest points to 9,115 feet (2,778 meters) at Rainbow Point and Yovimpa Point. Bryce Canyon is an International Dark Sky Park. Its night skies are protected so they stay clear and dark for visitors.

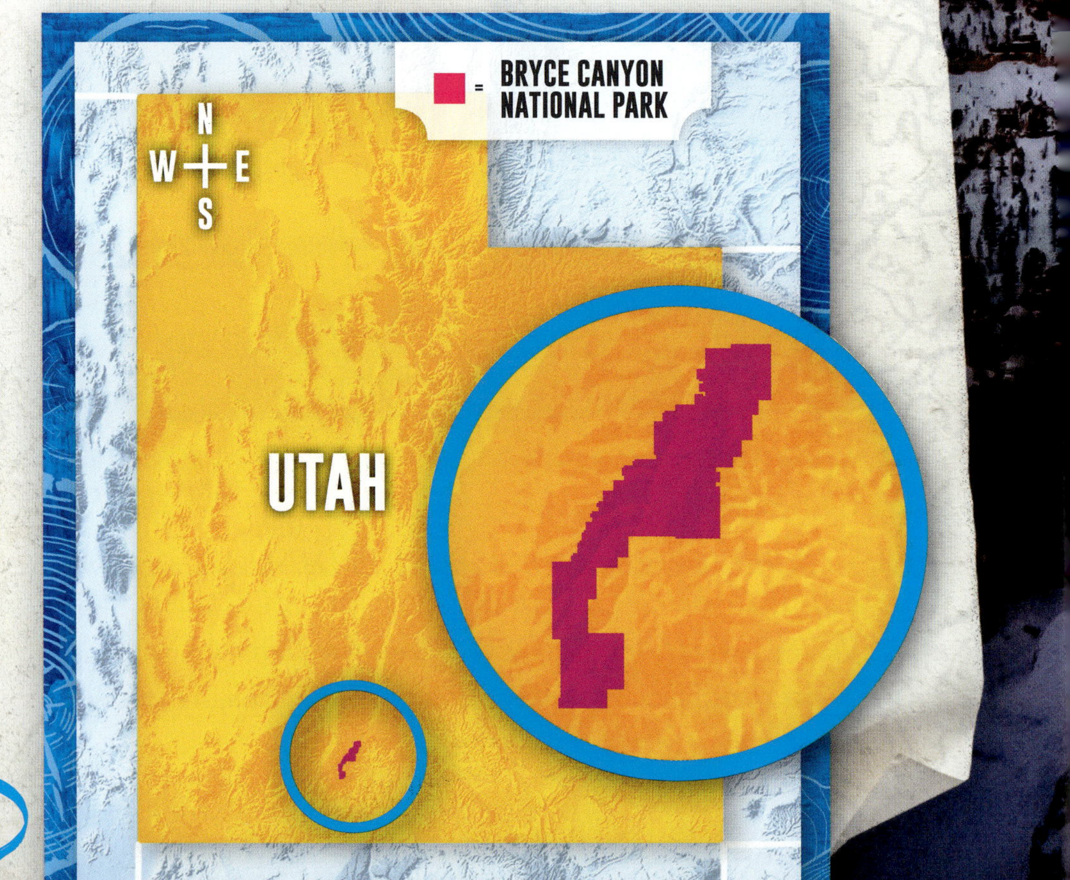

WHAT A VIEW

Bryce Canyon's many amphitheaters stretch over 20 miles (32 kilometers). Bryce Amphitheater is the largest. It is 12 miles (19 kilometers) long, 3 miles (5 kilometers) wide, and 800 feet (244 meters) deep.

THE LAND

Around 50 million years ago, a freshwater lake covered the area that is now Bryce Canyon. Over time, **sediments** washed into the lake and hardened into rocks. **Uplift** of the rocks caused plateaus to form.

Bryce Canyon often has warm days and cold nights due to its high elevation. Rain and melted snow seep into the plateau's cracks during the day and freeze at night. The ice expands as it freezes and splits rocks apart. This is called **ice wedging**. Over millions of years, ice wedging caused plateaus to break down to form hoodoos. This process continues today!

1. **Water seeps into cracks in plateau rock.**

2. **Water freezes and expands, splitting apart the rock.**

3. **Steps 1 and 2 repeat many times and the rock eventually breaks.**

Windows, or arches, are also found at Bryce Canyon. These rock formations are holes in rock walls. They are also formed by ice wedging. They can be seen atop the towering rocks called the Wall of Windows. Some windows are called bridges. Natural Bridge, formed from sedimentary rock, spans 85 feet (26 meters)! Over time, Bryce Canyon's windows will wear away and form hoodoos.

NATURAL BRIDGE

AVERAGE TEMPERATURES

JANUARY	APRIL
HIGH: 37°F (3°C)	HIGH: 54°F (12°C)
LOW: 15°F (-9°C)	LOW: 29°F (-2°C)

JULY	OCTOBER
HIGH: 80°F (27°C)	HIGH: 58°F (14°C)
LOW: 53°F (12°C)	LOW: 32°F (0°C)

°F = degrees Fahrenheit °C = degrees Celsius

Bryce Canyon has cold, snowy winters. Summers are mostly warm and dry. However, Bryce Canyon experiences a **monsoon** season during July and August. Afternoon thunderstorms with lightning are common!

PLANTS AND WILDLIFE

Bryce Canyon is full of wildlife! Utah prairie dogs dig homes in meadows. Pronghorns run through the park's northern fields. They easily outrun deadly mountain lions! Colorful paintbrushes bloom along trails. Butterflies fly among the flowers in warmer months. Willows grow near water.

Colorado pinyon pines and junipers live well at canyon bottoms. Their seeds and cones are tasty treats for mountain bluebirds and desert cottontails. Great Basin rattlesnakes slither between rocks. They shake their rattles to warn coyotes and hawks to stay away!

PRONGHORN

DESERT PAINTBRUSH

MOUNTAIN BLUEBIRD

GREAT BASIN RATTLESNAKE

TWO-TAILED SWALLOWTAIL

A FURRY GARDENER

Utah prairie dogs are only found in the southwestern corner of Utah. They add air to the soil when they dig their underground homes. This keeps the soil healthy and supports new plant growth!

UTAH PRAIRIE DOG

Life Span: around 5 to 8 years
Status: endangered

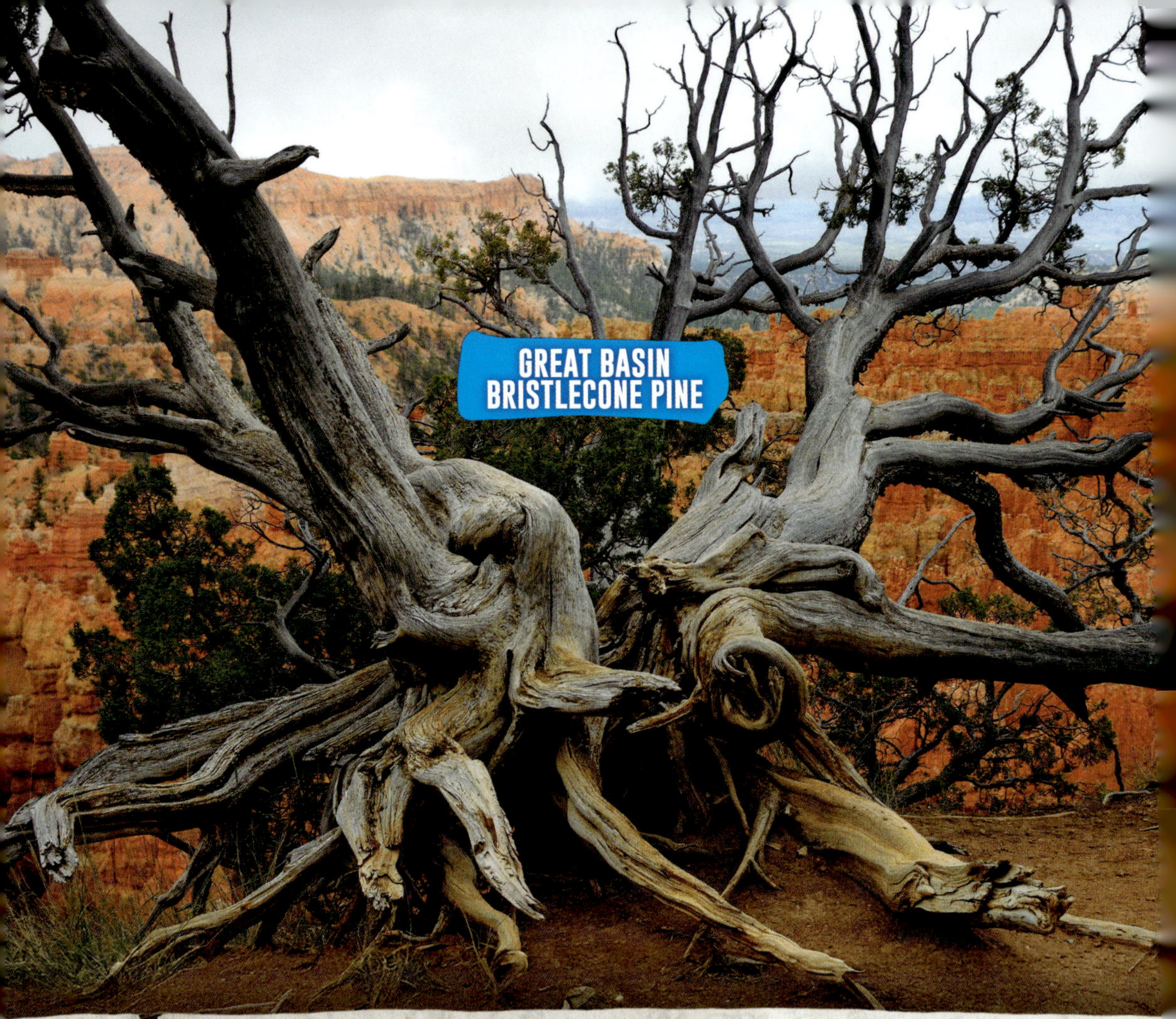
GREAT BASIN
BRISTLECONE PINE

Ponderosa pines grow throughout the middle elevations of the park. Pygmy nuthatches climb their trunks and branches to look for food under the bark. On the ground, mule deer snack on yarrow and bitterbrush. Squirrels scurry nearby.

PYGMY NUTHATCH

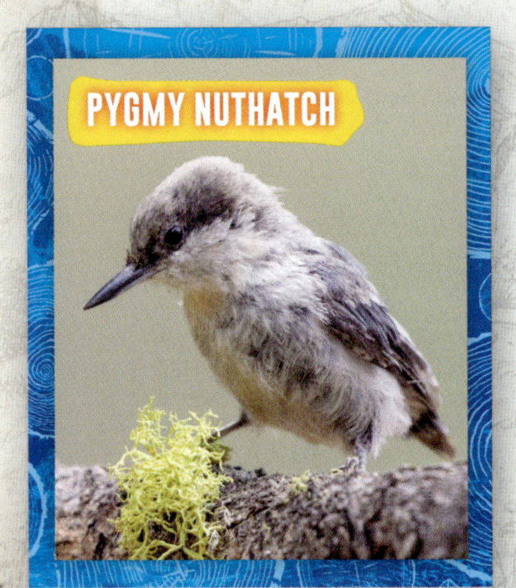

Coniferous trees stand tall at the highest elevations. They are homes for owls and Steller's jays. Peregrine falcons dive from above in search of prey. Near the rim of Bryce Canyon, Great Basin bristlecone pines thrive in the harsh weather. The oldest ones are around 1,600 years old!

PEREGRINE FALCON

Life Span: about 10 years

Status: least concern

peregrine falcon range=

LEAST CONCERN	NEAR THREATENED	VULNERABLE	ENDANGERED	CRITICALLY ENDANGERED	EXTINCT IN THE WILD	EXTINCT

HUMANS IN BRYCE CANYON NATIONAL PARK

People have **foraged** and hunted in Bryce Canyon for over 10,000 years. The Fremont people and the **Ancestral** Puebloans arrived around 200 CE. The Paiute first moved into the area around 1200. The Hopi, Zuni, Ute, and Navajo peoples also have ties to the land.

HOODOOS OR WHODOOS?

The Paiute people are known for a story about how hoodoos formed. It says that a god called Coyote turned "Legend People" into hoodoos as punishment for their bad behavior.

The Paiute people moved with the seasons. They gathered seeds and nuts. They hunted rabbits for meat and fur. They **traditionally** wove baskets with willows and made clothes with cliff rose bark. Stone and prairie dog bone were used to make tools.

Europeans began exploring the Bryce Canyon area in the 1770s as they traveled west. In the 1850s, **Mormons** arrived in search of farmlands. In 1874, a Mormon group built a town close to the area. Ebenezer Bryce and his family moved there in 1875. He built a road into an amphitheater to get timber. The locals called the place where the road ended "Bryce's Canyon."

Settlers forced the Paiute out of the area around the 1880s. But few new settlers came to the area. The harsh lands and long distance from railways kept people away.

EARLY HOME OF EBENEZER BRYCE

In 1915, a U.S. Forest Service worker named J.W. Humphrey visited Bryce Canyon. He was amazed by its beauty! He had photographs and films made of the area. These were sent to Washington, D.C., and the Union Pacific Railroad. Humphrey got money to improve the road so automobiles could reach the rim. In the1920s, the first lodge was built nearby. More people visited the area.

A HISTORIC LODGE

The Lodge at Bryce Canyon opened in 1925. It was declared a National Historical Landmark in 1987. This popular place has stood for over 100 years!

THE LODGE AT BRYCE CANYON, 1920s

Bryce Canyon became a national monument on June 8, 1923. It became Bryce Canyon National Park on September 15, 1928. Today, over two million people visit the park each year!

VISITING BRYCE CANYON NATIONAL PARK

Bryce Canyon attracts visitors from all over the world. An 18-mile (29-kilometer) scenic drive offers stunning views from nine overlooks. Hikers hit the trails to explore hoodoos and canyons. Some trails are easy while others offer a challenge! The "Hike the Hoodoos" program combines hiking with a fun search activity. In wintertime, rangers lead snowshoe hikes through deep snow.

SNOWSHOEING

RIM TRAIL

Stargazers flock to the park for its clear, dark skies. The park hosts a festival each summer that offers telescope viewings and other interesting activities during the day and night.

PROTECTING THE PARK

Bryce Canyon is threatened by **climate change**. This has caused the park to have fewer days with freezes and thaws. Without this freeze-thaw cycle, new hoodoos may not be able to form.

Air pollution from vehicles can make air, soil, and water dirty. This can harm the park's plants and animals. It also makes it harder for visitors to see the park's natural beauty. Light pollution is another concern. It affects animals that move and hunt in darkness. Nighttime light also impacts people's views of the clear night skies.

CARS ENTERING THE PARK

Bryce Canyon has a shuttle system to reduce the number of cars in the park. This helps lower its air pollution. The park has removed extra lights to reduce light pollution. Many outdoor lights now face downwards to reduce glare.

Visitors can do their part to protect the park. They should stay on marked trails and stay off hoodoos. They can respect the park's "Leave No Trace" rule and carry out all trash and food. They should also watch wildlife from far away. These efforts will help maintain the park's beauty far into the future!

PROTECTED WILDLIFE

Several types of animals that live in Bryce Canyon National Park are protected under the law. They include Utah prairie dogs, California condors, and southwestern willow flycatchers.

BRYCE CANYON NATIONAL PARK FACTS

Area: 56 square miles (145 square kilometers)

Area Rank: 50TH largest park

Date Designated:
June 8, 1923
(as a national monument)
September 15, 1928
(as a national park)

Annual Visitors:
2,498,075 visitors in 2024

Population Rank: 15TH most visited park in 2024

Highest Point: Yovimpa Point and Rainbow Point; 9,115 feet (2,778 meters)

TIMELINE

AROUND 1200

Paiute people move into the Bryce Canyon area

1875

Ebenezer Bryce and his family settle in the Bryce Canyon area

U.S. Forest Service worker J.W. Humphrey sees the Bryce Canyon area for the first time

JUNE 8,
1923

President Warren G. Harding declares Bryce Canyon a national monument

SEPTEMBER 15,
1928

The park becomes Bryce Canyon National Park

GLOSSARY

amphitheater—a rock formation made of flat or gently sloping areas surrounded by steep slopes

ancestral—related to relatives who lived long ago

canyon—a deep and narrow valley with steep sides

climate change—a human-caused change in Earth's weather due to warming temperatures

coniferous—related to trees and bushes that are evergreen, have needle-like leaves, and bear cones instead of seeds

elevations—heights above sea level

foraged—went out and searched for food

hoodoos—narrow towers made of rock

ice wedging—a process of breaking rocks apart by repeated freezing and thawing of water inside of the rocks

monsoon—related to winds that shift direction each season; monsoons bring heavy rain.

Mormons—members of the Church of Jesus Christ of Latter-day Saints

plateau—an area of flat, raised land

sediments—tiny pieces of rocks, minerals, and other natural materials; layers of sediments that are pressed together form sedimentary rocks.

settlers—people who move to live in a new place

telescope—related to a tube-shaped device used to see things that are far away, often in space

traditionally—related to customs, ideas, or beliefs handed down from one generation to the next

uplift—the act of causing a mass of land to rise

TO LEARN MORE

AT THE LIBRARY

Bowman, Chris. *Zion National Park*. Minneapolis, Minn.: Bellwether Media, 2023.

Oachs, Emily Rose. *Utah*. Minneapolis, Minn.: Bellwether Media, 2022.

Payne, Stefanie. *The National Parks: Discover All 62 Parks of the United States*. New York, N.Y.: DK Publishing, 2020.

ON THE WEB

FACTSURFER

Factsurfer.com gives you a safe, fun way to find more information.

1. Go to www.factsurfer.com.

2. Enter "Bryce Canyon National Park" into the search box and click 🔍.

3. Select your book cover to see a list of related content.

INDEX

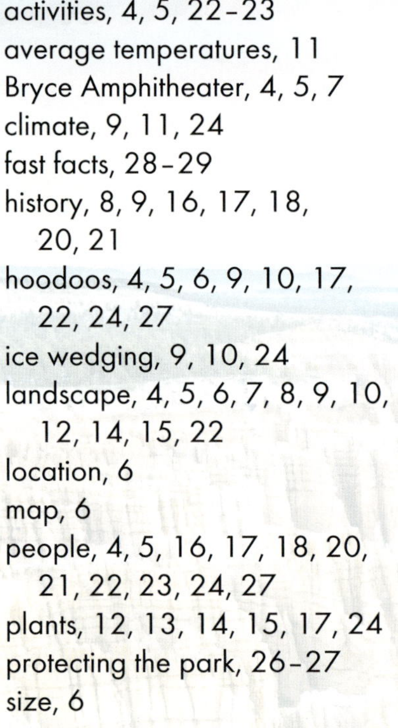

The images in this book are reproduced through the courtesy of: Rob, front cover; Yongyut Kumsri, p. 3; Sean Pavone, pp. 4-5; Nicholas J Klein, pp. 5, 22 (Natural Bridge); Ikunl, pp. 6-7; Alexey Stiop, p. 8; Ekaterina Pokrovsky, p. 10; Larry, p. 11; Jim, p. 12 (two-tailed swallowtail); Rod Gardner, p. 12 (pronghorn); Al Bittler, p. 12 (desert paintbrush); tomreichner, p. 12 (mountain bluebird); Breck P. Kent, p. 12 (Great Basin rattlesnake); Frank Fichtmüller, pp. 13, 29 (Utah prairie dog); Reinhard Tiburzy, p. 14 (great basin bristlecone pine); Janet, p. 14 (pygmy nuthatch); georgia.evans, p. 15; John Karl Hillers/ Wikipedia, p. 16; JFL Photography, pp. 16-17; George A. Grant/ Wikipedia, p. 18; jenifoto, pp. 18-19; NPS Photo (BRCA Archives)/ NPS, p. 20; photozims, p. 21; Kristi Blokhin, p. 22; Danita Delimont/ Alamy Stock Photo, p. 22 (snowshoeing); travellight, p. 22 (Thor's Hammer); Ian Dagnall/ Alamy Stock Photo, p. 22 (Bryce Point); dibrova, p. 22 (Inspiration Point); Eloi_Omella, pp. 24, 24-25; Red Herring, p. 26; Andriy Blokhin, pp. 26-27; Daderot/ Wikipedia, p. 28 (around 1200); Herb Bryce/ Wikipedia, p. 28 (1875); J.W. Humphrey/ NPS/ NPS, p. 28 (1915); Craig Zerbe, p. 29 (1923); Olga, p. 29 (1928); seread, p. 29 (mountain lion); Gabriel Cassan, p. 29 (coyote); Joshua, p. 29 (mule deer); Jared Quentin, p. 29 (bitterbrush); Matt Lavin/ Wikipedia, p. 29 (western wheatgrass).